MADE UP WI LIVERPOOL!

MADE UP WI LIVERPOOL!

A salute to the Scouse dialect

Ron Freethy

COUNTRYSIDE BOOKS
NEWBURY BERKSHIRE

First published 2007

COUNTRYSIDE BOOKS
3 Catherine Road
Newbury, Berkshire

To view our complete range of books,
please visit us at
www.countrysidebooks.co.uk

ISBN 978 1 84674 064 0

Both publisher and author acknowledge with gratitude the debt they owe to *Ey Up Mi Duck!* by Richard Scollins and John Titford, first published in 1976. That book was the inspiration for the series of regional dialect volumes of which this is one.

Designed by Peter Davies

Produced through MRM Associates Ltd., Reading
Printed by Cambridge University Press

All material for the manufacture of this book was sourced from sustainable forests.

CONTENTS

To friends I worked with on Radio Merseyside I acknowledge the help given by the station editor and, especially, Lynda McDermott, as together we explored the nooks and crannies of the area. To those who edited my recordings when I flew solo, I am forever grateful and to those many listeners who contributed so much to the content.

When working on a series called *Liverpool Wrecks* in the early years of 2000, I was greatly helped by Nigel Davies who was then working for the North Wales Tourist Board.

During the 1990s I exchanged much information about the North West with Cliff Heys who was born in Widnes and sailed most of the seven seas as a merchant seamen on cruise ships based out of Liverpool. It was from Cliff that I learned to give and take the Scouse humour.

At that time I was also writing and presenting programmes for Granada television, often in company with the late Bob Smithies. Together we made a one-hour documentary and numerous short films on the Mersey river and its catchments. I am ever grateful for the help I was given and the friendships I made at this time.

Whilst working on this book I have been given lots of help from journalists and friends not already mentioned and I am indebted to Paul Plunket, John Anson, Caroline Dutton and Librarian Danny Cleary, whilst Keith and Mary Hall helped me to source photographs. Thanks also to Emma Harrison and Sarah Hughes from Waterstones, Bold Street, who read the proofs.

Finally special thanks to my wife, Marlene, who worked wonders in typing Scouse dialect and to my son, Paul. He had enough contacts in the area and an appreciation of Scouseland that he encouraged me to write this book.

In the words of Scaffold pop group, 'Thank you very much .... Thank you very, very, very much ....'

To Arthur Dodd
Liverpool Coal Merchant

How strange to dedicate this book to a man who sold nutty slack in Knotty Ash! But Arthur Dodd gave us all his son called Ken. And, whilst Arthur carried coal to keep his local customers happy, Ken made a living from snuff quarries, jam butty mines and black pudding plantations.

Arthur was an entertainer and Ken followed in his footsteps. Ken deserved to receive the Bardic Crown for Rhubarb Bending and is a friend to all the Diddy-men who have delighted children of every age; a king of Scouseland, comic genius, and with his own entry in the *Guinness Book of Records*.

To father and son this book is humbly dedicated.

Treading for flatties in the Mersey estuary. The author on location for Granada TV, with Bob Smithies (right).

INTRODUCTION

My maternal grandfather was born and bred in Liverpool; he was a sailor plying the world but based in his native city. My paternal grandfather was a Cornish miner who had travelled the world mining tin, copper and, later, iron ore. Neither of these 'owd chaps' lost either their sense of humour or their accents until they day they died. I picked up words from both of them from the time I started to speak. I must be unique as I am a Cornish Scouser brought up in Cumbria!

After four years as a student in London, the Cockneys still could not understand me even though I later worked for the BBC and tried to speak 'proper like'. Later, I married a girl from Burnley and the language of the cotton mills was added to my vocabulary. Then came one of the most enjoyable periods of my life. I worked first for Granada Television, for whom I made programmes about the River Mersey. I

On 14th September 1957, the last tram rattled around Liverpool. This was my 21st birthday but I was then in the RAF, on Malta. Over the next week or two, I received three tram postcards; all sent to me by friends from the city who had rattled along the streets with me in our teenage years! I still treasure this memory.

was then involved with the Mersey Basin Campaign from 1985-2002 as a biologist helping to clean up the main river and its tributaries. These activities meant that I was in constant contact with Liverpudlians and found that words spoken by my grandfather were still being used.

In the mid 1990s I worked as a freelancer for BBC Radio Merseyside and my brief was to discover the heart of Liverpool, its buildings, its history, its food and its ambitions. I interviewed many Scousers and the rhythmic speech and fluent use of language never ceased to appeal.

When Countryside Books asked me to write this book about Scouse dialect, I hesitated – but not for long. Like all the others in what is a countrywide series, this volume is not meant just for pure bred Dicky Sams but also for Woolly Backed visitors to enjoy and help celebrate one of Britain's best known dialects.

I write this, with the wind in 'what's left of mi err', looking out at the River Mersey, which made up nearly ten years of my working life and I don't regret one minute of it.

Ron Freethy

CHAPTER 1

What is Scouse?

A book in the 1960s pointed out that there was a Lancashire dialect but it could not be distinguished from that spoken in Liverpool. The only conclusion from this is that the writer had never been to Liverpool and if he did risk a trip he would not be welcome.

Liverpudlians are better known these days as Scousers and they are fiercely loyal to their roots. They have one of the most distinctive dialects in the English language. Their humour is second to none and it is no accident, therefore, that some of the most famous British comedians have hailed from Liverpool (see chapter on Famous Scousers). Their humour is spontaneous and they are all masters of the ad lib. They poke fun at themselves and others, and very, very, few of these comedians have had confrontations with the censor.

Scouse-speak is like a butty, with the thick bread slices coming from Southport

Liverpool's waterfront.

In the 19th century, people poured into Liverpool in search of a better life.

speech on one side and the equally posh Wirral witterings on the other! The meat of the accent, however, is found in the heart of Liverpool itself and can be regarded as a mix of talk and song.

It is quite fitting that Liverpool was named the European City of Culture for 2008 because its speech contains elements of so many European languages.

The Romans arrived but very few Latin words entered our language at this time. The major shift came about with the Anglo-Saxons who penetrated the area from northern Germany and what is now southern Denmark and then, 400 years later, the Vikings, Norse and Dane who invaded northern parts from their bases in the Western Isles and the west coast of Scotland.

When William the Conqueror landed in Sussex, Norman French was then added to the mix and it quickly spread as the new masters of England removed the resident 'Saxons' from their lands and replaced them with the Norman friends of William.

The Normans were a religious, if warlike people, and they were so sure that their sins would find them out that they built churches and endowed abbeys which became rich and influential. There were splendid abbeys at Burscough, near Southport, Birkenhead and at Norton on the Wirral bank of the Mersey. The Saxon wooden churches already in the area were replaced by stone edifices with towers.

Despite the Norman influence, though, many Old Norse place-names do remain such as Kirkby, Ormskirk, Formby, Roby, and many others; *by* and *kirk* clearly show a Norse origin and so do many of the dialect words still used in and around Merseyside.

When King John established the port of Liverpool in the early 13th century, his intention was to use it as a base for invading Ireland. What has happened over the intervening centuries is that immigrants have poured into Liverpool, especially from Ireland in the 1840s when the potato harvest failed there and Scouse definitely owes its wonderful lilt to the Irish influence. Typical of Merseyside is that this influx of different people was achieved with little tension. Spud Murphy came to live side-by-side with Walter Welsh, Viking Victor, Saxon Sid and Norman Norman. Irish influences can be heard in words such as the plural of 'you' which becomes *youse*, e.g. *Are youse comin owt fer a bevvy?* One aspect which is prominent is the ending *-ck* as in ba*ck*s which should be pronounced as an 'x' whilst vowels become confused and a cat's *fur* and a fun *fair* are both pronounced as *fur*. In most of Lancashire, the word 'door' is pronounced *dewar*, whilst in Scouse this would be a sing-song like *dar* and reveals a clear Irish link.

Scouse obviously derives from the dish lobscouse that was cooked by sailors from countries such as Germany and Denmark. They called it *labskau*s and it was a broth of vegetables boiled up with any sort of available meat. It could include beef but was more likely to be offal, pigs' ears, trotters or tripe. The whole was thickened by grinding up dry ship's biscuits and adding them to the mix. In the days when the poor of Liverpool could seldom afford meat they made the broth anyway and called it *blind scouse*.

In these modern times a great fuss is made of standard spelling. Sadly, it does seem to be something that has become less important in schools these days, especially now pupils have access to computers which have a built-in *spol chick*. The great mistake with some of those who study regional dialects is that they insist that spellings should be rendered as they indicate. Try getting a Scouser to conform to anything by force and I will *eat hay wi a donky*. Either that or *I'll go a'ed to Formby beach an plat sand.*

CHAPTER 2

Scouse Humour

The inherent humour of the Liverpudlian people ensures that banter in the city is both personal and yet inoffensive. Even the buildings worshipped by architectural historians are given a comical accolade. Who, for instance, can blame those who, having looked at the shape of Liverpool's Roman Catholic cathedral, then give it the nickname 'Paddy's Wigwam'?

The celebrated architect Alfred Waterhouse, who was born in Liverpool and famous for his designs for Manchester Town Hall and Lime Street Station and Hotel, was also subjected to the 'Liverpool treatment'. His colleagues had nicknamed him Slaughterhouse Waterhouse because of his passion for blood-red terracotta brickwork. Scousers joined in the fun for almost as soon as it was unveiled, his Victorian clock tower on the University of Liverpool campus, funded by the Hartley's jam company, was christened the 'Waterhouse Slaughterhouse'.

Alfred Waterhouse's Victorian clock tower.

The world-famous Liverpool Philharmonic Orchestra was not immune either. Their new hall, built in 1939, with its magnificent acoustics, was said to be based on the design of King Tutankhamun's tomb and so was called locally Tut's Band long before the first concert was performed there. The Bryant and May match factory was the butt of Liverpudlians who worked at their poshly-named Diamond Factory – *Eer's a good match. My face and ewer arse.*

Even disasters can be lightened

Prime Minister Harold Wilson with members of The Beatles at the Show Business of the Year Awards 1964.

by the Liverpool humour. Compton Mackenzie's novel, *Whisky Galore*, set in the Hebrides and about a ship that went down carrying the 'staff of life' was based on a real event. The real ship was the SS *Politician* which had set sail from Liverpool, bound for Jamaica, but was blown off course and sank off the Scottish island of Eriskey. The comment when the book came out was, *That's nut th' only Politician wot got sunk i' the Pool.*

It goes without saying that many Liverpudlian politicians have a sense of humour. The heavyweight Labour MP Bessie Braddock, who represented Liverpool Exchange for 24 years, told of one of her 'run ins' with Winston Churchill during a late-night sitting. In the House, Winnie was slurring his words and Bessie stood up and shouted: 'You, sir, are drunk.' At which, Churchill replied, 'And you, madam, are ugly and in the morning I will be sober.' Bessie were a 'gam owd lass' and often told the story and added with a wicked grin 'We were both right'.

Another politician to take stick in Liverpool was Prime Minister Harold Wilson who was MP for the Merseyside area of Huyton. He was not helped by being born in Huddersfield in Yorkshire but like 'Battling Bessie' he held his own. He loved it when some wag from the hustings shouted out, 'We've niver 'ead o' Hitun' and followed this up by singing the rhyme,

Huyton, Huyton,
Two dogs a fighten.
Ones a black an'
Ones a whitun.

It is not surprising to find that the Liverpudlian humour as demonstrated by some of its finest comics is capable of being appreciated throughout Britain. Neither is it a surprise to find that Americans are seldom able to understand this form of often slapstick humour. Which American could possibly know what to do with Ken Dodd's tickling stick or deal with an attack from a band of Diddymen emerging from a snuff mine in the middle of Knotty Ash?

To be at Anfield as Liverpool fans sing *You'll Never Walk Alone* is one of the most moving experiences that anyone who loves sport can enjoy. But what about the humour from spectators and players alike?

There was a famous exchange between footballer Joe Mercer and a referee. Joe got on the wrong side of the ref whilst playing for Manchester City against Everton. Mercer, having got stuck in, was being reprimanded when he smiled at the ref and said,

'Wot wud you do if I called you a wassak?' (I've toned this down a bit!) *'I'd send you off'* replied the official. *'An wot if I only thowt you were a wassak?' 'I can't stop you thinking'* said the ref, knowing full well what to expect. *'Well I think you're a wassak'* retorted Joe. Both men went away laughing and the game went on with the crowd wondering what the joke was.

Whilst playing rugby a Scouser growled at me and noted my small stature. *'Wadda u 'ere for? Are you th' world's tallest midget?'*

Such is the Liverpool character that, after the game, he was the first to come up and give me a full pint of beer. He still buys me a bevvy whenever we meet and points out *'I dern't buy you a 'alf pint or yer'll duff me up'.* I couldn't *'cos ees sixfutseven'.*

This is Scouse humour at its best and totally devoid of malice; one of the best features of this wonderful city.

Opposite: Ken Dodd flying the flag.

CHAPTER 3

Famous Scousers

Liverpool is such a vibrant city that it was bound to breed comics with a unique brand of wit and wisdom. This should not hide the fact that here also were raised a variety of musicians: the Beatles, Cilla Black, Gerry and the Pacemakers and Frankie Vaughan, in the field of popular music; George Melly, the zany jazz musician; and Sir Thomas Beecham, one of the finest classical conductors of his age. Sir Thomas had a wicked sense of humour that shocked the serious establishment but delighted those who understood his wit.

Steven Gerrard, in action for Liverpool.

Once again, as elsewhere in this book, I have been forced to be selective knowing full well that I will be 'marmalised' (to quote Ken Dodd) by those who point out omissions. Those who make a study of the Scouse dialect and accent could do worse than listen to interviews given by famous Liverpudlian footballers including Ian Rush, John Aldridge, Michael Owen, Steven Gerrard, Jamie Carragher and, of course, the mercurial Wayne Rooney.

Some Evertonians have not forgiven Wayne Rooney for deserting the Everton

Blue for a Manchester Red. I once heard two Blues fans commenting when Rooney went down injured:

'I think ees pulled a muscle' said one.

'No he asnt' replied an unforgiving fan *'you cant pull bloody fat'.*

Arthur Askey

Big-hearted Arthur, born in 1900, became a major figure in variety, radio, film and, to some extent, television and was famous for his asides and ad-libs. His Liverpudlian quick-wittedness was seen at its best in pantomime and he starred as the dame Widow Twanky in *Aladdin* almost until his death in 1982.

In many of his films, the little feller was dwarfed by a 'tall brassy blond with the big boobies' called Sabrina. Arthur was never vulgar but along with Richard Murdoch in their radio programme, *Band Wagon*, the pair were masters of innuendo. This mickey-taking humour has always been typical of Merseyside:

'Where's your wife?'

'She's working on the Ferry. Th' whistles bust and she's providing the Mersey funnel.'

Dame Beryl Margaret Bainbridge

Born in Liverpool in 1932 and raised in nearby Formby, Beryl Bainbridge is a distinguished novelist and has been nominated several times for the Booker Prize. Her first book, *A Weekend with Claude*, was published in 1967 and her latest book *The Girl in the Polka Dot Dress* in 2007. In between these times she has had over 23 other books published, including *Young Adolf* and *The Birthday Boys*, a fictional account of Captain Scott's attempt to reach the South Pole._

Sir Thomas Beecham

Sir Thomas Beecham, the famous conductor, was born in St Helens in 1879. His grandfather had made his fortune from making and selling Beecham's Pills. They were *'nobbut a tanner but worth a guinea a box'.* Thomas himself had no need of the pills because he was a bundle of energy. He had a wicked sense of humour, too, although it was not appreciated by all. Once, when he was rehearsing a Christmas oratorio, a donkey on stage proceeded to pass water in the middle of a passage of music. Beecham looked up and said,

'It may be a poor actor but it's a bloody good critic!'

Alan Bleasdale

Born in Liverpool in 1946, Bleasdale qualified and first worked as a teacher before his illustrious career as a dramatist began. He wrote *The Black Stuff* which later developed into a TV series called *Boys from the Blackstuff* in 1982. Other award-winning TV dramas include *The Monocled Mutineer* in 1986. In 1999 Bleasdale adapted *Oliver Twist* for ITV. He has also been involved in musicals including '*Are You Lonesome Tonight*' and '*Anne of Green Gables*'.

Cilla Black

Priscilla Maria Veronica White was born to a devout Catholic family in Scotland Road, Liverpool, on 27th May 1943 – very much a wartime baby.

Although awarded an OBE, Cilla Black, as she later became known, has never lost her humility, her drive, her cut glass voice or her Scouse accent. In her singing career and later television work she has proved to have *a lorra, lorra talent* and has given *a lorra, lorra fun to a lorra, lorra people.*

Tony Booth

Tony Booth, the talented actor, was born in Crosby in the early 1930s. Although his long career has included films and the theatre, it is as the 'Scouse git' in the TV sit-com *Till Death Us Do Part*, with Warren Mitchell, Dandy Nichols and Una Stubbs, for which he is best remembered. He is also the father of Cherie Booth, QC, wife of former Prime Minister Tony Blair.

Tony Booth and Una Stubbs in the TV sitcom, Till Death Us Do Part.

The young Cilla Black.

Two awestruck children looking at the grave of the Childe of Hale.

The Childe of Hale

On a recent visit to the grave of John Middleton, known as the Childe of Hale, I overheard two Liverpool children pointing at the last resting place of this most famous resident of Hale village, now close to the John Lennon airport:

> *'Ee's 'uge he is – he's bigger then mi grandad.'*
> *'I'll bet ee et a lot.'*
> *'So does mi grandad – an' he smokes fags!'*

John Middleton (1578-1623) is said to have been 9 ft 3 ins tall and built of such proportions that he became a famous wrestler. In 1604 Sir Gilbert Ireland, Lord of the Manor of Hale, was invited by King James to take John to London to wrestle with the king's mighty champion. After demolishing the king's favourite in short order and collecting his prize of twenty guineas, John Middleton was sent home to avoid further embarrassment to the monarch. The Childe's life-size portrait hangs in a room at Brasenose College, Oxford, and a copy of it can be seen at Speke Hall, within walking distance of the Hale cottage where the giant was born and which still exists.

All we can say is that this was 'no mere child'.

Ken Dodd

When coal merchant Arthur Dodd and his wife produced a lad to be called Ken on 8th November 1927 they little realised that he would make their Liverpool suburb of Knotty Ash famous. When he was young he fell off his bike and ever afterwards his teeth protruded, but this only helped to add to his distinctive look when he became a comedian. Diddymen, tickling sticks, coil oil and nutty slack were local terms which he worked into his act. His ad libs and unique sense of humour were obvious and his stage stamina is legendary. He has entered the Guinness Book of Records for the longest joke-telling session – 1,500 jokes in 3½ hours – but his lyrical tenor voice also became well known. Between 1960 and 1981 he produced a series of hit singles, including *Love Is Like A Violin, Tears* and *Hold My Hand.* If these were treated seriously by pop music lovers, the same cannot be said for his rendering of *Where's Me Shirt?* which is full of Scouse fun.

I once heard him ad lib outside a theatre when asked by the waiting crowd to sing. Doddy began, 'My new tune is dedicated to the only decent pub in Manchester'. He then sang *Love Is Like A Vile Inn.*

Billy Fury

Ronald Wycherley born in Dingle, Liverpool, in 1940, worked as a deck hand on the Mersey tug boats. But music was his great love and he got his big break with the impresario Larry Parnes. His name was changed to Billy Fury and he went on to have a string of hits on the Decca label, with songs such as *Halfway to Paradise* which climbed to number 3 in the music charts. Considered to be one of the finest male solo artists of his generation, Billy suffered a fatal heart attack in 1983. His life is still celebrated through his fan club and the many tribute acts that perform his songs. A statue of him by Liverpool sculptor Tom Murphy stands in Albert Dock.

Gerry and the Pacemakers

Born in Liverpool in September 1942, Gerard Marsden formed a group in the early 1960s, along with his brother and others. Like the Beatles, the Pacemakers were managed by Brian Epstein and, for a time, were serious rivals to the Fab Four.

Gerry and his group will be forever famous in Liverpool because it was they who recorded the Rogers and Hammerstein tune *You'll Never Walk Alone* which echoes around Anfield each home game and which the fans often sing at away matches as well. The group's *Ferry Cross the Mersey* was a hit in 1965 and was followed by a film of the same name.

William Ewart Gladstone

This stubborn old Scouser, born in Rodney Street, Liverpool in 1809, dominated politics in Victorian England from the time that Robert Peel and then Lord Derby realised his worth. His only rival was Benjamin Disraeli. To begin with both men were Tories but when Gladstone defected to the Liberals the battle lines were drawn. Gladstone served as Prime Minister four times between 1864 and 1894.

His home estate was at Hawarden on the Welsh border with Chester. One of his charities was engaged in the setting up of hostels for fallen women. I once heard a joke in a Liverpool pub,

> *'Ee was a good fella, were Gladstone. He wonce saved a wummen fer mi grandad but it cost towd fella a tenner.'*

Tommy Handley

Tommy Handley, born in 1892, sadly had a short life, dying from a brain haemorrhage at the age of 56. He was famous for keeping up the nation's spirits during the dark days of the Second World War. His radio programme called *ITMA* (*It's That Man Again*) poked fun at Fumf the spy, Mrs Mopp the char lady whose catch phrase was 'Can I do you now sir?' and a pessimistic lady called Mona Lott. There were *a lorra others* and *ITMA* hides the fact that Tommy Handley began his career in light opera and was well known for his rich baritone voice.

Carla Lane

Born Romana Barrack on 5th August 1937, Carla has to be regarded as a very loveable and talented eccentric. She eats, breathes and sleeps animal rights but her

Tommy Handley. It was his being so cheerful that kept folk going during the Second World War.

talent as a scriptwriter shines out. Who else but a Liverpool lass could have written the TV comedy programmes *The Liver Birds* and *Bread*, both of which show Scouse speak at its best and most humorous.

Roger McGough

Born on November 9th 1937, McGough should be regarded as a serious poet. He went to Hull University, where he came under the influence of Philip Larkin. His early fame came as he performed with the humorous pop group, Scaffold, whose other members included John Gorman and Mike McGear, brother of Paul McCartney. Scaffold's version of *Lily the Pink* topped the charts in 1968. Roger also wrote some of the lyrics for the Beatles' animated film *Yellow Submarine*.

Meanwhile, he was becoming well known as a poet and, along with Adrian Henri and Brian Pattern, produced a book of poems called *The Mersey Sound*. He reads his works in public and his soft Scouse accent is ideally suited to these performances.

Jimmy McGovern

Born in 1949, Liverpudlian McGovern has become one of the most prominent television scriptwriters of recent years. He first worked on *Brookside* in 1982 and in 1993 he created the award-winning TV series *Cracker*. He also wrote a dramatic reconstruction of the 1989 Hillsborough disaster which was screened by ITV in 1996. In 2004 he wrote *Gunpowder Treason and Plot* and, in 2007, completed a work called *King Cotton* which will play regularly as part of the 2008 European City of Culture event.

George Melly

Born in Liverpool in 1926, Alan George Haywood Melly came from a well-to-do family and was educated at Stowe College. It was here that he became an accomplished musician specialising in jazz and blues. Sadly he died in 2007 but he was always true to his roots and his autobiography was entitled *Scouse Mouse*.

I once met him during a wet and windy test match at Lords when he looked a treat in his striped blazer and an umbrella that had blown inside out.

'I got these togs from a deck chair on New Brighton beach' he said as he dumped his brolly in a bin. 'This bloody thing is wrecked just like the Dockers Umbrella back home!'

Tom O'Connor

Here is a gentle, humorous man in all senses of the word who was born in Bootle in 1939. He attended St Mary's Grammar School and went on to become a teacher of art and mathematics in Liverpool before embarking on a show business career. Tom's Scouse humour has always been close to the surface and he made his name in TV performances such as *The Comedians.*

Like most Scouse comics, O'Connor is never vulgar but always bubbling over with energy and wit. Here is no 'bozzle-eyed blasphema' but a Scouser with his eyes focused on fun. He has proved a highly successful all round entertainer in his own shows, as a quiz master, and more recently, as a regular guest on *Countdown.*

Paul James O'Grady

Born in June 1965 in Birkenhead this superb comedian and drag artist worked as a clerk in a magistrate's court and in an abattoir just by way of a contrast! He then travelled widely taking jobs as a barman, including one stint in a brothel in Manila. It was here that he fashioned his character Lily Savage and converted her into the celebrated Scouse tart.

His versatility is wide and is still being explored, to the delight of TV audiences.

Ted Ray

Born Charles Olden in Wigan in 1905, the comedian known as Ted Ray can be classed as a Scouser because the family moved to Liverpool when he was just three weeks old. His jokes were sometimes awful but his delivery was beautiful and his claim to fame was pretending to play the violin very badly – no mean feat. His sons Robin and Andrew became excellent musicians in their own right. His *Ray's a Laugh* was a popular radio show in the 1950s. He was also a very good golfer and this caused some confusion because there was a professional golfer of the same name.

Jimmy Tarbuck

Tarby was born in 1940 and went to the same junior school as John Lennon – not a bad pair for one school! Jimmy was the last host of the theatre run called *Sunday Night at the London Palladium* and became a household name for quiz shows like *Winner Takes All.* Like Ted Ray, Jimmy Tarbuck is a more than average golfer and a fanatical supporter of the game.

Frankie Vaughan

The voice and the stage act of this consummate performer became a byword for song and dance sophistication at his peak during the 1950s and into the late 1960s. He was regarded as a 'ponsy Southern softie' by many but how wrong they were. Frank Abelson was a Jewish lad born in Liverpool in 1928 who won a scholarship to the Lancaster School of Art where his voice was noticed as he sang with the academy dance band. At this time Frank was highly regarded as a boxer and about

Lily Savage (Paul O'Grady) and George Melly on stage.

to turn professional. His nimble footwork learned in the ring was soon adapted to the 'sexy shuffle' so typical of his act. He continued working into the 1980s and died in 1999.

Joseph Williamson

Before the Mersey Tunnel was built, Joseph Williamson, born in 1769, had his own 'tunnel vision'. He made his vast fortune from tobacco and snuff, with huge factories close to the Liverpool docks. But why did he pay men to dig the huge network of caverns under the Paradise Street area of the city? Most think that it was to provide work for them during the recession following the end of the Napoleonic Wars in 1815. Since 2002 the Joseph Williamson Society Trust has restored the tunnels which had long been used as refuse dumps. A part of the network is now open to the public and is becoming an unusual tourist attraction.

The Beatles

The last word on famous Scousers should, of course, go to the Beatles as it was the Fab Four who made Liverpool renowned all over the world. It is still a mecca for pop fans everywhere.

John Lennon, Paul McCartney, George Harrison and Ringo Starr are too well known to be documented here but in the case of the first two their former homes are now looked after by the National Trust; and the Beatles Experience Museum on the Pier Head is always crowded with eager visitors wanting to know more about the group and the celebrated Cavern Club.

One wonders which fame came first. Did the Beatles make Liverpool or did Liverpool make the Beatles? This is a bit like the result of a game between Liverpool and Everton – *yer allus get sumat owt o'a drawer.*

The wealth of musical talent bubbling out of Liverpool shows no signs of stopping. The Beatles have been followed by innumerable pop and rock bands, including Frankie Goes to Hollywood and Echo and the Bunnymen, two very successful groups. OMD, another Liverpool band, still attracts large audiences and boasts great recording sales. The Cream Nightclub has become the Cavern of its day. The all-girl band Atomic Kitten has also exploded onto the music scene.

New poets will be inspired by Roger McGough, writers like Brian Jacques will continue to inspire children, whilst comedians with their own brand of humour will appear from time to time. Scouse and Scousers will always make waves in the sea of success.

Glossy and Frazes

Many people think that we need to preserve our dialects 'unspoiled' but they do not appreciate that our speech is evolving all the time. The Merseyside language is ever-changing. It has been so since the time when immigrants began to enter the port from the 18th century onwards. There were Irish, Scots and folk from the Isle of Man and, in recent years, the Chinese community has been augmented by people from Eastern Europe. Scouse talk is part of our history and should be preserved and passed on from mouth to mouth! This dick-shoo-nary is meant to help.

addick watter poor quality beer. It meant literally haddock's water which was what remained when fish had been boiled.

akker to stutter.

ale ouse a pub: *I'll get the beers in, yewer ale ouse or mine?*

ali gents' hairdressers - *Looke at yer 'err. Get youse to see Ali.* (Rhyming slang – Ali Baba)

anti-quack old-fashioned, antique.

arse board the part of a cart nearest to the horse.

aul old. With a 'd' added this obviously becomes old and many a young person refers to their father as 'me aul man' and his mother as 'me aul gerl'.

bag'ed someone under the influence of drink or drugs.

bail, to go to run away.

Bally Ann Day A time when all scraps of food were mixed together and eaten because there was 'bugger all' left in the larder!

base van a police van covering close circuit television cameras and now part of the surveillance of Liverpool's night life. *Oerr – she wus overnite in th' base van.*

beak 1. a judge or magistrate. 2. a drug, especially cocaine. *Lookattim – ees beakfodder 'ee is.*

beechamed taken a remedy: *Wait a bit whacker – you'll be fine now yoov bin beechamed.* The St Helen's company, Beecham, has been famous for its pills and potions since Victorian times.

bevvy, bevvied alcoholic drink, drunk. *One mare bevvy and I'm off* means one more for the road.

bezzie best: *bezzie mate.*

biffta a poor person who is not very bright; also slang for a cigarette. The anti-smoking laws which came into effect in 2007 probably mean that someone who lights up a *biffta* in an *ale ouse* is a bit of a *biffta!*

binnie dustman.

bizzie a policeman, see also **scuffer**.

blert an idiot: *Gerroff don' be a gret blert.*

Blue Nose a supporter of Everton Football Club.

A statue of legendary Dixie Dean stands outside Goodison Park, home to Everton Football Club.

bomby to bomb. First used in the Blitz of 1940: *Aye mate it were ruff. We got bombied three times at home and a th' docks.*

bommy a bonfire.

bonechute the mouth. *Shut yer bonechute.*

boxer coffin maker. My grandad once said to me that 'Auld Thexton' is a boxer and I'd have a scrap with him soon. We thought the 'owd fella' had gone ga-ga because Thexton was an elderly, tubby chap. Then I discovered he was the undertaker and realised that Grandad *werenut reet weal.*

bozzle eyed cross eyed. Bozzle eyed Bessie from Toxteth was a pawnbroker who handled taxed (stolen) goods.

brassy (blonde) a prostitute.

bucko a pugnacious type. Someone always spoiling for a fight who would rather *ave a fight than his dinner.* The word probably derives from Spanish. Spanish sailors who enjoyed a fight onshore called themselves *vaqueros* which in English became *buckeroos.*

butty a sandwich.

cackhanded a clumsy person or, more usually, a left hander. A practical joke in the shipbuilding trades in Liverpool was to send new apprentices to the stores for 'cackhanded screwdrivers'.

can lad the youngest employee whose job it was to brew the tea. *Its nowt to do wi mee – I'm ownly th' can lad.*

Catlicker a Catholic.

chewey chewing gum.

casey a leather football, with a bladder inside it, which could be laced up. The modern football is now a marvel of technology and much lighter. Bill Shankly, the legendary Liverpool manager, said of his early playing days in the Glasgow tenements: 'We were so poor we kicked cans into goals made up of piles of rubbish. There was no way we would afford a *casey*.'

cheggie a chestnut. Either a horse chestnut conker, or a sweet chestnut still served occasionally and prepared on charcoal burners.

At Liverpool's ground, stands a statue of Bill Shankly, one of the greatest football managers of all time.

chincough a persistent, hacking cough or a cold. Posh folk would say, 'Don't sit on that cold wet bench, you'll become ill' whilst the Scouser would be more direct, *Gerroff that cold spot, you'll soon have chincough in your arse and its ewer own daft fault.*

chief 1. the boss: *Now pin back yer lug oles chief an' listen ter me.* 2. to steal: *Som buggers chiefed me wotch.*

to have a cob on 1. to be in a sulk. 2. to create a scene, having 'lost one's rag': *Tek no notice o err – she's gorra a cob on.*

codzedid having a mouth as big as a fish: *Oerr heres codzedid.*

coil oil literally, 'coal hole', a cellar or coal house. At one time, most houses had open fires and a visit to the coal man was an important event. Folk would 'copper up their money' and decide how many bags could be *bunged in th' coil oil.*

cozzy bathing costume of the old woollen type which often became heavy when wet. *Mi cozzy were ringing wet for ages when I came owt. I were bloody freezin.*

deawdle 1. to dawdle, move slowly. 2. to be pessimistic: *Don't sit there deawdlin, get yer arses into gear.*

Dicky Sam used to describe someone born and bred in the city. The term evolved in the 19th century and is still used in

Liverpool today. *Oh himm hes a real Dicky Sam from way back.*

dipper a pickpocket. Visitors are still warned about being *dipped,* especially at sporting events such as Grand National meets at Aintree.

dishwasher a pied wagtail.

divvy slow thinking. *Tek no notice er him, he's a divvy.*

Dockers' Umbrella nostalgic name for the overhead railway which used to operate in Liverpool. It opened in 1893 and was described as 'the first railway in the sky'. The busiest year was in 1919 when nearly 20 million passengers were carried along the 6½ mile track. There were stations at Seaforth Sands, Gladstone, Alexandra Brocklebank, Canada, Huskisson, Nelson, Clarence, Princes, Pier Head, James Street, Canning, Wapping, Brunswick, Toxteth, Herculaneum and Dingle. It was a sad day for the city when the Umbrella was demolished in 1957.

The Dockers Umbrella in the 1940s.

dog shelf — the floor.

Dolly Varden — the night soil cart. Dolly Vardens toured the city collecting human excrement. These carts were then emptied into ships (one was called the Sir Robert Fowler!) and the night soil was taken out and dumped at sea. When Charles Dickens dreamed up Dolly Varden for the heroine's name in his novel, *Barnaby Rudge*, he can never have visualised how her name would be taken in vain!

Doris — an affectionate name for an old lady – *She's mi aul Doris.*

duffin — a beating: *Ey lukerim ees ed a great duffin.* Also *hidin*, equally common.

edge pig — a hedgehog.

erdoo — a hairdo: *Looker err, she's ad a new erdoo.*

faff — wasting time – *Quit faffin aroun' an' do sum werk.*

farrantly — 1. quickly: *Don't 'ang abaht usedo it farrantly.* 2. well-behaved or good-looking: *She's a reight nice farrantly Doris.*

firebobby — a fireman, whose vehicle was often called a *firebobby bus.*

frozzed — very cold.

ganzy — jumper, jersey or pullover.

gegging — interfering, nosey.

git — dopey, not very bright.

glory oil — a space, usually under the stairs, where clutter can be stored. Originated in the days of steam ships when a door was opened to shovel coal into the boilers.

gozzie eyed — having a squint. At one time it was chanted at those children who were unlucky enough to wear glasses. *Eer cums gossie eyes* was a frequent taunt used by playground bullies.

grock — 1. a deposit of phlegm stuck in the throat. 2. more recently, a big, bossy person (also **grockle**).

hessian — bucket. In the 18th century, leather water buckets were called hessians because they resembled the shape of boots worn by military regiments from Hesse in Germany. In the 1770s the quality of water was so bad in Liverpool that carriers brought in supplies and sold it from hessian-shaped leather buckets. This cost as much, if not more, than a similar measure of beer.

Hey, lads, hey Get a move on. The expression dates back to the time when criminals were being chased and the police used this cry in the same way that foxhunters shouted 'Tally ho'. These days it is used to gee up a flagging individual or team.

hottie a cooling tower.

I'll go ter th' top of ower steers an expression of surprise. Well, I never!

irnins wages.

jerry built badly built. This is said to derive from a Liverpool firm called Jerry Brothers, Builders and Contractors, who built houses of poor quality during the late 19th and early 20th century which attracted buyers or renters from the working and lower middle classes.

jigger the back entry to a street of houses.

jigger rabbit an alley cat.

Jinny Greenteeth a water goblin who would swim up the Mersey to deal with unruly and mucky kids.

judy attractive young lady.

keks trousers.

kidda an affectionate name not only for children but also used for a favourite friend: *Tell yer wot kidda, I'll buy th' next round.*

kipper a two-faced and gutless person: *Ees a kipper hoo needs a duffin up.*

kittying washing. Kitty Wilkinson was born Catherine Seaward in Londonderry in 1786. When she was young, her family set out to seek a new life in Liverpool. The ship was wrecked on the Hoyle Bank and her mother and sister were drowned. From the age of 12 she was sent to work in a cotton mill at Caton. She married a sailor who died leaving her to bring up two small children alone. She returned to Liverpool and campaigned for improvements to hygiene in the city. Thanks to her the first municipal wash houses were set up on Upper Frederick Street and, hence, working-class women went to this laundry to do their *kittying*.

larmy alarm clock.

larrop a slap.

larropin a beating: *Use shurrup or thal git a larropin.*

leccie electricity: *O er, she add ter fiddle th' lecciemeter.*

leg it to run away.

liver bird a cormorant. The bird standing proudly atop the Liver Building on the Pier Head is not a mythical one but has been recognised by ornithologists as an accurate depiction of a cormorant carrying a beak full of seaweed. This bird is one of the most common species to be found diving for fish in the Mersey estuary and holding out its wings to dry in the wind. It builds a bulky nest of seaweed so the statue is very accurate.

One of the famous liver birds.

lodge box a radio. Named after Sir Oliver Lodge (1851-1940) who was the first professor of physics at the University College Liverpool. He was a pioneer in the use of radio and some think he may have got there before Sebastian Ziani de Ferranti (1864-1930) who despite his name was also born in Liverpool. So the next time you turn a lever or a knob, or press a button to select a station, or even press a button, remember that the frequency changing operation was invented by Lodge.

lug ole literally, ear hole; the ear: *Shut up yews bonechute or nextl'cum a clip on th' lug ole.*

lurcher a thief.

marmalised mugged.

medicinal compounds

A brew used to induce an abortion. The Scaffold song *Lily the Pink* has a meaningful line about Aunty Millie going round 'dispersing her medicinal compound which was the saviour of the human race'.

made up very, very pleased. *Me an our kid were made up when th' Pool won the League and we did th' dubble gen Everton. We rubbed their toffee noses in th' mud.*

mizzle gentle rainfall or heavy mist.

moonlightin moving house without paying the rent.

motty 1. a share: *Come on whack, you ev to stick yower motty* which means placing drinking money into a central kitty.
2. interfering: *Look ar err, she's always stickin err motty in.*

mouldy warp a mole (the burrowing animal).

nob 'ead an idiot. This was used in an offensive way to indicate that the person had made a mistake and the fault was emphasised by tapping the fingers on the head and pointing at the miscreant. *Skon 'ead* has a similar meaning.

ornpipin dancing: (from 'hornpipe').

ollies, ols holidays: *I'm on me ols.*

ozzie a hospital.

paddies' tranquilliser
a policeman's truncheon.

penguin house a convent.

poke sack.

potato a hole in a sock.

Prodigers Protestants.

pud wood in th' ole close the door.

puke young child.

puntin' to have a bet.

rabs sports shoes.

riveted married. Obviously comes from an old ship-building term.
Av been riveted ter th' gel fer nearly forty yers.
Yer'd get less fer murder.

scally an untidy looking youth (shortened version of scallywag) The untidy looking mops were thought to be reminiscent of the greenery sticking out from spring onions. Many shoppers in these areas still ask for a bunch of 'scally onions'.

scons head: *I bumped me'ed. Me scons still urts.*

scrat end a burned chip. *Fish 'n' chips and chuck in a few scrat ends* was one order which was usually agreed to by chippies who wanted to keep valuable customers.

scratting hard up. *I'd like ter go on me ollies but I'm scratting for th' cash.*

scuffer policeman (see also **bizzie**). A not so polite name but a well known term at the time of the classic TV series, 'Z Cars'.

skelpt punished: *Gerroff or yuel get skelpt.*

skuwel school.

shabby a starling.

sithers scissors.

shooting gallery a toilet: *Sorryiselate. Gotstuck i' th' shootin gallery.*

snaffle to steal.

snaffler a person who is economical with the truth and who cannot be trusted. Such people often *snaffled* other people's property. Sports teams which scraped a victory were often said to have *snaffled* a win.

sneck a door latch.

snig an eel.

snotty snobbish – *she dunt fancy us. Snotty cow, err is.*

snozzle the nose: *Lukeris snotty snozzle.*

sound 1. a good idea. 2. a respected friend.

spends pocket money: *Youse stopit oruse I get nospends.*

spink a chaffinch.

tatty 'ed someone with a very scruffy haircut. Don't look at a smooth easy to peel potato bought from a supermarket but look at a seed potato and turn it upside down to reveal its gnarled stems which later develop into tubers. Then you can call an untidy kid a 'tatty 'ed'.

to tonk to strike hard: *Lukerim, he got tonked.*

twirlie too early: *Sorry I missed th' bus. We've not gorra lorra time but I'm sure that bloody bus were twirlie. Cum in even if thas twirlie* often greets one who arrives ahead of time.

ugly mug originally a member of a club formed in Liverpool in January 1743. It was given the grand title of Ye Most Honourable and Facetious Society of Ugly Faces – definitely Liverpool humour at its very best. To be accepted into the club, members had to be ugly enough to qualify; bad teeth, bozzle eyes and stinking breath were measured. Good-looking people were black balled.

The club only lasted for eleven years but it was led by John Wood the Elder of Bath, who designed the attractive Liverpool town hall. Old-time Scousers still invite people they can joke with to join the Ugly Mug Club and are prepared to buy them a supply of Ugly Pills to make sure they gain membership!

Liverpool town hall, designed by the founding member of the 'Ugly Mug Club.'

Vatican the Scouse name for the new VAT offices built in the city.

whacker a close friend. It probably has its origins in pea whack, a thick soup which was almost the staple diet of the Liverpool poor during the late 19th century.

whaky baccy cannabis: *Scuffers gorim wi whaky baccy.*

widdlehouse a gents' urinal.

woolly back an outsider. A term used by 'true Scousers' to describe those of their friends and enemies who do not have the privilege of being born and bred in Liverpool. This term is often applied to Manchester United fans but with a few added embellishments!

writing lark a yellowhammer.

youse plural of 'you': *Gerroff youse lot.*

CHAPTER 5

Scouse Scoff

Scouse obviously derives from the dish of the same name that was cooked by sailors from Germany and Denmark who visited the port of Liverpool. They called it *labskau*s and it was a broth of vegetables boiled up with any sort of available meat. It could include beef but was more likely to be offal, pigs' ears, trotters or tripe. The whole was thickened by grinding up dry ship's biscuits and adding them to the mix. It was nutritious, cheap and easy to cook, even at sea when the weather was rough. It was not just the sea that was rough, though, so was life for the Liverpool poor who seldom could afford to buy meat. They made the broth anyway, though, and called it *blind Scouse*.

Many of the recipes listed here ought to carry a health warning because they should be cooked in fat. The healthy option is to use vegetable oil but the old Scouse way is to cook in beef dripping. This is still produced by Parry Scragg Limited of Liverpool whose origins go back to 1825. The firm began on Carruthers Street near the city centre and there was a Scragg at the helm until 1972; then came a merger with the Parry family three years later.

The menus which follow have been 'tarted up' but would still be recognised by Scousers of more than a century ago who liked to enjoy the taste of their food even if it was cheap. And the answer to those who grumble about unhealthy foods is that there is an easy solution – lick your lips, plug up your lug oils, and eat less of it.

Asparagus and shrimps

These days this is regarded as an up-market and expensive starter to a posh meal but, in former days, during the peak of the season, the poor of Merseyside had both these delicacies available locally. Supply and demand meant that in seasons of 'glut' such foods were cheap. So it was with asparagus and shrimps.

From early times asparagus was recognised as a healthy vegetable. It has a pleasant flavour and the stems contain a mild diuretic. It is native to the Mediterranean and was an early introduction to the port of Liverpool. *Asparagus officinalis*, as it is scientifically known, grows only in light sandy soil and it soon became an important crop in the area between Liverpool and Southport. This is still the case today and is much in demand during its short harvesting period.

Shrimps used to be caught from small fishing boats with a shallow draft so that the fishermen could trawl their nets close inshore. These vessels were called nobbies and, in the late 19th century, there were upwards of one hundred nobbies working between the Mersey and the Ribble. Shrimps can still be caught locally but the process of catching, cooking and shelling is so labour-intensive that they are expensive.

Method

Place the asparagus stems into boiling water for 2-3 minutes before removing and draining. Put these on a plate and cover them with shrimps. Drizzle over these a dressing of mayonnaise or mint sauce. Serve immediately with a few slices of brown bread.

Clout Pudding

This is a cheap Merseyside equivalent to a Scottish haggis. First take a clean cloth called a clout and dust it with flour. Fill it with a mixture of animal fat or Parry Scragg's dripping, into which can be added anything which needs eating up. Nobody wasted food in the old days. Savoury clout might have included meat (if you were lucky) and chopped vegetables. It used to be a tradition to visit a market as it was closing, especially on Saturdays, and buy up what had not been sold.

Sweet clout would involve using treacle or fruit that was becoming past its best. The clout was tied up and placed in a pan of boiling water. When ready, this dish was a variation of our modern broth and dumplings, and it is still a favourite winter warmer in our house.

Everton Toffee

Those with a sweet tooth and a love of the traditions of football continue to celebrate the name of Everton, one of the founder members of the football league and whose team are still known as 'the toffee men'.

Prior to the spread of Liverpool, Everton was just a village set on a hill on the outskirts of the city. It was then a lung for many Liverpool folk intent on a breath of fresh air. It was a popular walk up to Everton where they would treat themselves to the sweetmeat which had been perfected by Molly Bushell in 1753. She kept her recipe a secret to ensure that her profit margins remained as high as possible. An image of one of the original buildings in Everton where the toffee was made still adorns the Everton football strip.

Nowadays, the toffee is made by the Liverpool company Barker & Dobson and encased in a minty striped coating and known as Everton mints. A less well known secret concerning Scouse sweets is that Barker & Dobson were the first to make boiled sweets and wrap them individually; an hygienically sensible example of the packaging which is now such an unwanted feature of our modern life!

Fish and Chips

It is said, probably with some truth, that the first fish and chip shop was opened in Oldham around 1880. In some coastal areas, including Southport and along the Merseyside coast, fishermen took along their own fish to their local chippie for it to be cooked. The shop deep-fried it in animal fat and charged for this service. Chips were sold to go with the fish and the whole meal was sprinkled with lashings of salt and vinegar, and then wrapped in newspaper. How unhealthy and unhygienic! What lovely grub!

Some people would buy their fish direct from the inshore nobby boatmen who, in the Southport and Formby areas, had their own sales outlets in the form of fishing stalls that were pegged out on the beach.

Flatties

Liverpool began its working life as a tiny fishing village. All the best fish would be sold to the posh people. There were, however, some flat fish which were so small that they did not have a significant market value. Such little 'flatties' were dabs,

Flatties and tatties.

flounders and tiny plaice. These were grilled and served with boiled nettles chopped up with butter or dripping and eaten with a thick slice of home-made bread.

The dab (*limanda limanda*) is a small flat fish seldom growing to more than 16 inches (40 cms) or weighing in excess of 2½ pounds (1.3 kg). Mostly they are much smaller than this and are typical by having dark backs and white bellies. This shows that they are bottom living and do not need to waste resources by producing pigments on the belly. They can be caught on hooks, in nets and even by visiting pools after the tide has ebbed and feeling them with your bare feet as they wriggle under the sand. This is called 'treading' and I have enjoyed this type of fishing during most of my life. You can, of course, also buy them from the supermarket quite cheaply.

Tatties

Potatoes were first brought to England from the New World in the 16th century and were said to be an aphrodisiac. Initially, they were very expensive and were first grown commercially in the Formby area and near Ormskirk around 1680. It was soon discovered that the local soil was ideal for growing 'spuds'. A further advantage was that the tubers were full of carbohydrate and were very easy to store. As the population increased, the potato proved to be the best or, should it be, the cheapest, food for the poor. A Liverpool market trader once told me of a conversation she had with a customer:

'Is them tatties local?'
'Yes.'
'Weer from?'
'Preston I think.'
'That's not bloody local. That's ten miles away. Have you got no Ormskirks?'
'These are fresher.'
'Aye but they're not local. I'll ga someweer else and get locals.'

Method

Dabs – 1 to 3 per person depending upon size. Place the dabs on a grill pan or on a barbeque frame after coating them with oil or butter. A little garlic can be added if required. The dish should be served hot, with salt and vinegar added, but another variation is to serve with parsley sauce and a chopped onion. Pickled onions can also be added as a garnish.

For the chips, use large potatoes so that they can be sliced easily. These are often called scallops when so prepared. Either immerse the slices into hot fat as they are or, as an alternative, coat them in batter and then fry them.

Lips and Lugs

These days I buy 'pigs ears' as a special treat for my Labrador and it was only recently that I realised what an old Liverpudlian meant by a dish called 'lips and lugs'. In the days when butchers killed and cut up their own beasts not a lot was wasted. The cheaper offal was sold for human consumption and not converted into pet food as is the case today.

Pigs' ears and the fleshy areas around the mouth would be boiled up until really soft and then mixed with stale bread (if there was any) and served as a broth. Brains of animals were also used and this is still a delicacy today in parts of Australia. Yes, really! The Aussies will forgive me for pointing out that the convicts around Botany Bay would have known of the 'lips and lugs' in the days before the Scuffers transported them.

Pan Heggerty

I have known this dish ever since I started eating solid food some 70 years ago. I still have my mother's recipe which is as follows:

1 pound of potatoes
1 onion
rashers of bacon (quantity depending on your finances)
pepper

Method

Fry the bacon a little, just to release the essential fat. Then take out the bacon and put it to one side. Cut the potatoes and onions into very thin slices and place into the frying pan, arranging them in layers. Fry gently until cooked and then place the bacon on top. The final touch is to brown and crisp the bacon under the grill.

Pan Pie

One of my very earliest memories was sitting at my grandad's feet with the family dog curled up beside me, gazing at the old black leaded stove and waiting for my pan pie. In later years, people came to hate these old ranges and replaced them with gas or electric cookers. Confined for many years as museum pieces, they are now commanding high prices as people who can afford them want a touch of nostalgia. They usually have a modern cooker, in addition, though!

Grandad had worked in the boiler rooms of steam ships all his life whilst away at sea so he knew well how to make up a fire that would boil water and heat pans by pushing coals into the cavity beneath an oven.

I waited patiently for my pan pie and the dog called Zebo also looked on expectantly. Zebo was as 'black as th' fire back' and took his name from the one on the tin of black lead which grandma used to keep the range in tip top trim.

This dish was usually eaten on Monday, as a cheap way of using up any mutton left over from the Sunday meal.

Ingredients
left-over meat
1 large onion
4 medium-sized potatoes
1 pint of water
seasoning
pastry rolled up to make a lid

Method

Chop the meat into small squares and the same with the onion. Slice the potatoes. Fill a saucepan with the seasoned water and add the meat, onion and potatoes. Cover with the pastry and cook on the hob for about 20 minutes. The pastry lid is like one continuous dumpling.

Samphire

Many recipe books praise samphire, the name of which is said to be a corruption of St Peter (Pierre) the patron saint of fishermen. Where it grows on sea cliffs, it is known as rock samphire, and is distinguished by its fleshy green leaves which can be preserved in vinegar.

Samphire to a Scouser, however, refers not to this plant but to marsh samphire or 'glasswort'. This, too, is excellent to eat and has been economically important to the Liverpool area for centuries.

In the 1980s I made a television film on the coastline between Hale Point and Liverpool, an area famous for its chemical industry, particularly glass which is still important around St Helens. I gathered some marsh samphire and divided my crop into two piles. The first pile I mixed with sand in a fireproof container and placed this on a driftwood fire. Two hours later I had a few bubbles of glass and, hence, the name 'glasswort' was entirely obvious. The rest of my samphire glasswort I washed in a flask of cold fresh water and then placed into a beef sandwich. It can also be served hot by gently warming the plant in a dish of butter with lots of black pepper. Salt is not needed as the glasswort is already salty. Served with freshly baked bread and a glass of chilled white wine it is delicious.

Some of the local hostelries serve it with Southport shrimps and it is equally enjoyable. However, you could quite easily ignore the white wine and substitute a dark frothy glass of Cains beer. The old mariners knew that samphire was good for you. Also growing on the seashore was a plant known as scurvy grass. This is related to watercress and contains lots of vitamin C. It was used to keep scurvy at bay before it was discovered that lime juice prevented the disease and the Yanks learned to call us 'Limeys'.

Scouse

Obviously this was a popular dish in the area and there are many variations. The choice of meat can vary but families often joined together and shared the left-overs of a roast.

Ingredients
4 large potatoes
4 large carrots
beef and/or neck of lamb
2 onions
stock (could be an Oxo cube) made up to one pint
seasoning

Method

If using uncooked meat, toss it in seasoned flour and brown quickly in a frying pan to seal the juices. Cut the potatoes into large chunks and chop the carrots and onions. Place the meat, potatoes and carrots into a saucepan; add the stock and seasoning. Simmer for two hours and keep stirring regularly during the cooking. Add more flour paste to thicken towards the end of the cooking. If you have no meat you could *mek a do weyout and hev blind scouse*.

Snig Pie

From the 1820s there was a thriving eel fishery around the Mersey and at Widnes there was once a pub called Snig Pie House which was *full ter bustin speshially on Whit Monday wot were then called Snig Monday.*

The eels were cooked in butter or dripping and served beneath a thick brown crust.

Wet Nelly

This is not the name for a lass emerging from the Mersey with a drippin' cozzie but a rather calorific if cheap pudding. It was popular in Liverpool until the Second World War and in some of the poorer areas it was popular until the 1960s. People would queue at their local bakers as the shop was shutting and buy up any cakes

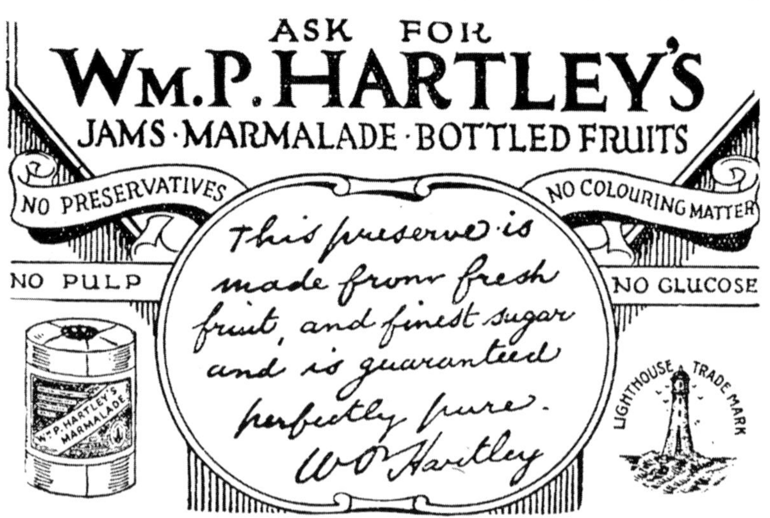

HARTLEY'S JARS

All Hartley's Jars are made to average full weight, but Jam will evaporate during storage. To lessen that risk, we fill into our jars every year hundreds of thousands of pounds more Jam than we actually charge for.

TABLE JELLIES

HARTLEY'S TABLE JELLIES are pure, wholesome and transparent. Of delicious flavour, yet reasonable in price. They are an ornament to any table and palatable to the most refined taste.

SAUCE

HARTLEY'S SAUCE, prepared from the very finest selected fruits and spices, is a most delicious and appetising thick sauce.

HARTLEY'S FACTORIES are built on model lines, and each process in all their departments is carried on under absolutely perfect conditions.

WM. P. HARTLEY, Ltd., Aintree, Liverpool

Hartley's jam was just what you needed to make Wet Nelly.

that were left at knock down prices. So-called *stales* were even cheaper. These were broken up and warmed with treacle or syrup. Many Liverpool cake shops make and sell their own 'wet nelly' but nowadays it is a rather more upmarket food, mixed with dried fruit and baked in an impressive looking pastry.

Whitebait and Onion Rings

These days we visit smart restaurants and order whitebait as a starter. These are the young of herrings and sprats. Served on a garnished platter of freshly-prepared salad, with a slice of lemon, the dish looks, and is, expensive. There was a time, though, when this kind of dish was a very cheap meal for *them as cud nor afford big fish* around the Mersey catchment.

Warrington in the 19th century was famous for its food including potatoes, damsons and gooseberries but especially for its smelts and sparlings which until pollution killed off the catch afforded a very lucrative living for the Mersey boatmen.

Whitebait are lightly fried in dripping (these days in a more healthy vegetable oil) after having been dusted with breadcrumbs. Cut an onion into slices and pull these apart. Wrap the strips of onion around the fish either before cooking or after as a fresh garnish. Care should be taken not to overcook the whitebait otherwise it becomes rubbery.

Cains beer

No Liverpudlian lad would dream of going into his local if it did not serve Cains beer. It has been brewed in the heart of the city since 1858 and the firm has a right to be proud of being designated the Beer of the Year for the celebrations surrounding the city becoming the European City of Culture for 2008. Those who want to try out any of these recipes may want to enjoy a glass of Cains to go with their food.

In the mid 19th century Liverpool was a busy port and a very thirsty place. Robert Cain, an Irishman from County Cork was determined to make his fortune and began to brew his own ale in his own pub. Some seven years later he bought an old brewery site on Stanhope Street and his beer became so famous that he was able to build more than 200 pubs designed to a high standard. In 1887 he built a brand new brewery and its ornate tower is still a major landmark in Liverpool today. Robert Cain died in 1907, aged 81 but his name and his beer lives on.

CHAPTER 6

All at Sea

From its origins as a tiny fishing village, Liverpool, with the Mersey estuary currents stirring up the sand, has developed steadily into the city and port which we all know and love. There have, however, been periods in the history of Liverpool which have literally been watersheds.

When King John set up the port around 1210, his idea was to use it as a base for expanding his dominions into Ireland but it was not until the rise of the cotton industry in the 1780s, when trade with America and the West Indies grew, that Liverpool became a major trading port. Apart from the cotton, tobacco and sugar that passed through the port, Liverpool, sadly, was also a significant player in the slave trade.

The approaches to the port can be treacherous and Liverpool Bay has become famous for its wrecks. Three of these: the *Royal Charter*, the *Lelia* and the *Resurgam* are of particular significance.

In her day, the *Royal Charter* built in Liverpool was the fastest and most luxurious passenger ship afloat and plied the route to and from Australia. Most of the incoming passengers were rich and had their luggage loaded with Australian gold. In late October 1859 the *Royal Charter* was only a few hours away from the safety of Liverpool when it was struck by a storm of massive force. She sank in the area of Moelfre, in North Wales, with the loss of 450 men, women and children, plus an unknown quantity of gold bullion and coins. Some of these recovered gold coins and artefacts are on display in the museums of North Wales and Liverpool and are a sad reminder of this tragic event.

During the American Civil War, Britain ostensibly was neutral but Liverpool had close ties with the Southern States through the cotton trade and many of the Confederate steamships were built in the city. The *Lelia,* built by Millers of Liverpool in 1864, sank in Liverpool Bay, supposedly loaded with coal and iron ore. In reality, though, she had American Confederate officers on board and her holds contained powder, ammunition and thousands of rifles.

In my opinion, the Yanks are still being unreasonable in casting doubts on this innocent and inoffensive coal ship. After all she only had in her holds ten thousand Enfield rifles, one million percussion caps, three thousand cavalry sabres, one

Poster advertising the Royal Charter *which sank just before reaching her home port of Liverpool.*

Captain Arthur Sinclair of the Confederate Navy who was aboard the Lelia *when she sank. His body was washed up at Fleetwood and identified by his watch which he had bought in Liverpool.*

thousand short rifles with cutlass bayonets and four hundred barrels of gunpowder! There were a few other bits and pieces plus uniforms of Confederate blue but what a fuss to make about such a trifle!

Even this diplomatic storm, though, paled into insignificance compared to the *Alabama* fiasco which soured relations between Britain and the ultimately victorious Northern States for more than a decade. The *Alabama* was built by Cammell Laird, a ship building company set up in 1824 by William Laird. She sailed from Liverpool to join in hostilities and sank 50 Union vessels between 1862 and 1863. After being almost continually at sea for two years, the *Alabama* was in need of a refit but, whilst en route back to Liverpool, was sunk off the French coast in June 1864 by the United States steamship *Kearsage*. In 1873 the US Government demanded that the British pay them the then enormous sum of £3 million in compensation for allowing the Confederate States to purchase ships in England and allowing them to use British ports. This resulted in Laird, by then the mayor of Birkenhead, not getting the knighthood for which he had been strongly tipped.

Another fascinating link between Birkenhead and the American Civil War is that the Confederate flag, hauled down from the mast of the Confederate steam ship

The world's first working submarine, the Resurgam.

Shenandoah when in the Mersey for a refit on 10th November 1865, was the last Southern States emblem to be struck; so the hostilities ended not in America but on the waters of the Mersey!

Modern submarine history also began in Liverpool Bay in 1879. The *Resurgam* was built by Cockrane and Company of Birkenhead and was 45 ft long and with a 9-ft beam. She was wrecked and sunk on 25th February 1880. One of the most exciting days of my working life was being taken out into Liverpool Bay to watch an echo-tracing of the *Resurgam* lying almost intact on the seabed. She looked like a can of beans with pointed ends rather than flat. and I listened to plans to lift and restore her. What a world famous exhibit this would be!

Another almost, but not quite, forgotten aspect of Liverpool's heyday as a port was the age of the Transatlantic liner which was in full swing from the 1880s until just after the Second World War. American film stars en route to promote their movies (which in Liverpool were called *fillums or flicks*) would disembark and shoals of photographers waited at the gangplanks to snap them. They would then follow these celebrities, usually to the Adelphi Hotel, and then onto the station at Lime Street for the steam train to London.

Many of the liners carrying these movie stars were built by Cunard and a look at the Cunard building on the Pier Head reveals how prosperous the company became. Cunard made handsome profits but had to withstand rivals from Germany and France and especially from the White Star Line which also operated out of Liverpool and Southampton. One of the most famous Cunard vessels was the *Lusitania* which was sunk by German U-boats in 1915. She had been built in 1906, the same year as her sister ship, the *Mauritania*, and which from 1907 to 1929 held the Blue Riband for the fastest Atlantic crossing. Both Cunard liners, the *Queen Mary* and the *Queen Elizabeth*, built in the 1930s, were converted into troop ships during the Second World War. After peace, they were refurbished and again attracted the rich and famous but sea travel began to lose out to air travel at the end of the 1950s.

There is still a small market, though, for ocean cruising for pleasure, based out of Liverpool, and with air travel currently presenting well publicised problems, the popularity of this type of holiday seems likely to increase. In the 1970s the *Ocean Monarch* cruises did a roaring trade and it is still hoped that 'Fly and Cruise' holidays may be replaced by 'Cruise and Cruise' variations.

Without any doubt, the transatlantic crossings represented the most famous period when Liverpool was 'all at sea'. But although we should remember the 'play'

Liners built by local yards like Cunard sailed out of Liverpool on a regular basis.

Much of Liverpool's wealth in the 19th century derived from the cargoes that passed through its magnificent docks.

we must not forget the 'work. Liverpool Docks still handle more tons of goods today than ever before though this involves far fewer ships, which are unloaded not by hundreds of dockers but by a highly mechanised system of cranes from sealed containers.

We should also remember the hundreds of small sailing ships which once weaved their way into the Albert dock system and think of the thousands of sailors from all over the world who sought refuge in Liverpool and the army of strong muscular dockers who literally manhandled the cargoes. These tough chaps were seen at their bravest and best during the war when they unloaded food, armaments and huge crates containing sections of aircraft. They watched the Atlantic convoys set off to face the Blitz from the air and U-boats from under the sea.

The cornerstone of Liverpool's maritime history must be the magnificent docks which were so profitable in the days of sail. The mouth of the Mersey provided a quicker passage to North America and, as the focus of trade shifted from the European ports to the Atlantic ones, Liverpool soon outstripped Bristol as the premier west coast port.

Jesse Hartley who was the dock engineer from 1824 to 1860 devised a system of interlinking docks which were connected by an ingenious series of locks. This became the first enclosed dock system in the world and, in 1846, Prince Albert, the consort of Queen Victoria, opened the first dock. He was able to tour the system on board the royal yacht, the *Fairy*.

By the 1960s the Albert Dock was all but derelict but then the system was restored and converted into a shopping centre with pubs, restaurants and museums. It is now composed of the largest group of Grade I listed buildings to be found in Britain and can be explored on foot or, better still, from the little pleasure boats which not only tour the docks but which can become amphibious, sprout wheels and do tours on land!

The regenerated Albert Docks.

Statues and Buildings

Here in Liverpool is one of the most historic dockland areas in the world and there are more splendid Georgian terraces in Liverpool than there are in Bath. Following the Georgian success, this proud port continued to be at the forefront of architectural design into Victorian times and followed on with the Three Graces on the Pier Head. No wonder therefore that Liverpool was designated the European City of Culture for 2008.

The city is also rightly proud of its two cathedrals: the Anglican cathedral which was designed by a Catholic and the Roman church designed by a Protestant.

The city's international flavour is underlined by the fact that the Chinese area of Liverpool was the first of its type to develop in Europe whilst Americans and especially the Irish added to this glorious mix. On the other side of the river the Wirral which is still a proud part of Merseyside has its own wonderfully varied culture with Celtic (Welsh and Irish) and Norse influence to the fore.

To make a selection from Merseyside's marvellous buildings and statues is not easy and there is no doubt that future generations will add their own imposing monuments.

Aintree

Without any question, the Grand National is the most famous horse race in the world. A chap called William Lynn built a grandstand on land he leased from Lord Sefton and staged the first race meeting at Aintree in 1829. And, in 1837, Lord 'Dashalong' Sefton himself organised an event in the Maghull area to race horses from one church to another which is where the word 'steeplechase' originated.

Aintree's fame has duly attracted crowds of bookmakers, touts, punters and tipsters, the most famous of these calling himself Prince Monolulu. My grandad was a keen horse racing fanatic (which was why he was so poor) and my father followed in his footsteps with an equal lack of success. Both knew of the Prince. He would stand up at Aintree wearing a top hat and shouting, 'I've gorra n'orse' and would whisper the name of the winner to those who would part with their hard-earned cash. With his prominent local accent we must assume that his only claim to royalty was to be a prince of tipsters.

The Liverpudlian comic Freddie Starr and his horse, Minnehona, celebrate winning Aintree's famous race, the Grand National, in 1994.

Although long dead by then, no doubt the Prince would have tipped Red Rum, who finished runner up in the National twice and won the race three times! Red Rum was a real king of Merseyside and was trained on and around the Southport sands which are hard enough to cope with at the gallop.

Anfield – The Home of Everton F.C.

Before any fan of the Red half of the Pool sends me a death threat, let me prove my point. I need to explain what a Blue Nose was once doing in the Red zone.

The team we now know as Everton and a founder member of the Football League in 1888, began in 1878 as St Domingo's church team. Their first venue was Stanley Park, now situated between Anfield and Everton's present ground at Goodison. Bootle was then the main team in the Liverpool area but Everton soon took over. In 1889 they developed a new ground at Anfield. Everton had just celebrated winning the League Championships in 1891 when their landlord increased their rent so much that they abandoned Anfield and built a new ground at Goodison. The landlord himself took umbrage and formed his own club which he called Liverpool.

No wonder the clubs are still fierce rivals!

The Baltic Fleet

Anyone who wants to experience the flavour of Liverpool as a major seaport should visit this wonderful traditional old pub. In the days of sail, the Baltic Fleet was a haunt of sailors who plied to and from the Baltic area where the cargo was mainly of timber which was in short supply in Britain during the 17th and 18th centuries.

Sit in the pub, taste the traditional food and sample the real ale which is actually brewed on the premises. You can enjoy a drink and take in the smell of malt at the same time.

Birkenhead Park

As the city of Liverpool expanded, a regular ferry operated across the Mersey which meant that, for a few coppers, families could cross over to the Wirral and enjoy the open spaces there. One of the favourite places to stroll was Birkenhead, with one of the most famous parks in the world.

It was laid out in 1847 by Sir Joseph Paxton, who was well known for his design of the Crystal Palace in London. Paxton's assistant for the Birkenhead project was a chap named Hornblower and I often wonder if this name inspired the hero in the novels by C. S. Forester. What is more certain is that Birkenhead Park was visited by Americans who returned home, put pressure on the authorities to copy the design, and laid out Central Park in New York.

Birkenhead Priory and the Tunnels

When the Benedictine monks founded Birkenhead Priory in 1125, they were allowed to set up a ferry system using rowing boats. The tolls they collected made the abbey rich. It is interesting to note that we now have two Mersey road tunnels but the tolls are still collected on the Wirral side. Thanks to Henry VIII not much of the abbey remains and it is now swamped by Victorian buildings but it is open to the public. On entry, monastic plainsong replaces the hum of traffic and visitors are transported back over centuries of proud history.

When the first Mersey road tunnel was opened on 18th July 1934 by King George V, it was the longest underwater *roadoil* in the world at 2.13 miles. The second tunnel dates to 1970 and is 1½ miles. For a while it was known as *th' numbertwooil.* Together, these tunnels have relegated the Mersey ferries to operating just a pleasure trade but thankfully it is still very much a feature of a tradition going back around 600 years.

Two Cathedrals

There is no city in the world that I know of which has two huge cathedrals so close together. The Anglican and the Roman Catholic edifices look well enough on their own but when viewed together from above the Mersey they are indeed a very pretty pair.

Both are modern but in terms of age the Anglican pile comes first. The building, designed by Giles Gilbert Scott at the age of only 22, was begun in 1904 but was only finally completed in the Gothic style in 1978 when it was consecrated in the presence of Queen Elizabeth. It is the fifth largest cathedral and the largest Anglican church in the world. By some distance it also has the largest and heaviest peal of bells in the world. The stained glass alone is worth a visit and not only depicts religious scenes but also celebrates the lives of prominent philanthropic citizens of the city.

The Roman Catholic Metropolitan Cathedral of Christ the King was designed by Edwin Lutyens and the first stone was laid in 1933. Building work was disrupted by the Second World War, however, and it only opened for business in 1967. Like the best of red wines, it has needed time to mature and has now taken its place on the world's architectural stage.

Opposite page: Liverpool's Anglican cathedral and (below) the Catholic cathedral fondly known as Paddy's Wigwam.

Eastham Ferry and the Double Pub

In the days before the Mersey road tunnels, travellers had to use the boat ferries which left from a number of piers along the Wirral bank of the river. One of the most important of these was at Eastham. When the weather was rough, though, travellers had to wait to cross and a hotel was provided for the 'quality' to rest and wait. Their coachmen and servants could not use this facility and so had their own hostelry. Two hostelries from this era which have survived, are the Eastham Ferry Hotel and the Tap. The remnants of the old ferry can still be seen and a country park has been built around the area, with well marked footpaths. If you want posh nosh, try the Eastham Ferry, whilst you can enjoy a good bevvy at the Tap.

Florence Nightingale Memorial

The lady of the lamp has a Liverpool memorial to her but this should really be shared with a lady called Agnes Jones who, despite her surname, was an Irish woman. Having trained at the Florence Nightingale nurse training school in London, she travelled north in 1865 to become Superintendent of the Liverpool Workhouse. This workhouse was one of the largest in Europe and a most unhealthy spot. Agnes was also put in charge of the newly-established local training school for nurses that had been set up with the help of the great Liverpool benefactor, William Rathbone. He had sought the advice of Florence Nightingale as to how to set up such a school. The advice he received and which was implemented by Agnes was so valuable that not only was the health of the inhabitants of the workhouse improved but it led to the first District Nursing Service being established on Soho Street.

Florence deserves her memorial and so does the Irish Jones who is commemorated in one of the stained glass windows in the Anglican cathedral.

King's Pipe

The Stanley Dock, set at the terminus of the Leeds and Liverpool Canal, became the largest bonded warehouse in the world. Large consignments were stored until the appropriate duty was paid. Sometimes a company would not pay the dues and in this case their stock was burned, along with damaged goods like tobacco. The chimney associated with the boiler soon became known to Liverpool folk as the King's Pipe and can still be seen on Great Howard Street.

Lewis Jones Memorial on Pier Head

Sir Alfred Lewis Jones (1845-1909) deserves his monument erected on the Pier Head in 1913 for his pioneering work in setting up the Liverpool School of Tropical Medicine which is still run as a charity to this day. Sir Ronald Ross, the first lecturer

Pier Head from the Maritime Museum.

of tropical diseases at the school, was awarded the Nobel Peace Prize in 1902 for his work in linking malaria with the female mosquito and this was supplemented by other works discovering the agents causing elephantiasis (the skin hardening disease) in 1900, sleeping sickness in 1901 and tick fever in 1905. The school is still a world leader and obviously developed because of Liverpool's position as a major seaport.

Jones began his working life in the shipping office of the Elder Dempster Fishing Line and it was the steamships which brought the first bananas into Britain. It was soon realised that the banana was a very important health food and we should thank Sir Alfred Lewis Jones each time we peel one!

The Magazine

This is a pub on the Wirral Bank, near New Brighton, that stands on what was once an isolated site where gunpowder stores were located in the days of sail. On their way out to sea the sail-powered warships known as the 'Ships of the Line' called in briefly here to fill their magazines. The pub still serves hot food, but not that hot, and some of the old powder storehouses remain to this day.

Nelson's Memorial

It is quite right that a city as important as Liverpool should celebrate the victories of Lord Nelson and there are two memorials to Bozzle Eye's exploits – *oneagood* and *wunabadun*.

The first and, by far the tallest of the two memorials, was built to represent an Egyptian stylus with the *aul lad issell* perched on top. It was sited in the area known as Exchange Flags. In the days of sail, ship owners could see Bidston Hill on the Wirral side of the Mersey. They could focus their telescopes on flags placed on the hill and read the signals and anticipate which ship was about to come into harbour. However, the structure was not popular and was moved and re-erected in Springfield Park, close to the Alder Hey Children's Hospital.

The second memorial, which stands behind the town hall and is at the centre of Exchange Flags, is much more impressive. This was the first of Liverpool's sculptures to be paid for entirely by public subscription and depicts not just Trafalgar but other important victories at Copenhagen, St Vincent and the Nile. Part of Southport is still called the Nile to this day.

The land victory at Waterloo is celebrated by the Wellington Memorial situated near Lime Street railway station.

Otterspool

This is just what this area was at one time – an otter's pool. From the car park, picnic site and pub, a 2-mile stroll on the promenade leads to the museums and the Pier Head.

The place, however, is rubbish! At one time, before the days of planned landfill, this bank of the river was the municipal rubbish dump. From around 1930 until its completion just before the Second World War, the mud, rock and other debris from the Mersey Tunnel was conveniently dumped at Otterspool. During the war most of the rubble from the Blitz was spread among the rest of the rubbish. Afterwards, the area was landscaped and a solid promenade was built. This area was the proud focus for the International Garden Festival which was held in Liverpool in 1984.

Developments associated with the European City of Culture status have 'tarted it up' and it is now once more a pretty spot.

Perch Rock Fort and New Brighton

Perch Rock Fort was built in 1825 from the red sandstone typical of this stretch of the Wirral and was provided with around one hundred Vickers Armstrong cannon designed to protect the entrance to Liverpool Bay. A lighthouse was built at the same time and sailing vessels were obliged to pay a sixpenny toll to receive this 'guiding light'.

The guns were fired only once in anger when they engaged either a U-boat or a floating log during the First World War. In 1958 the War Office decided to sell the fort and after a period of neglect it has now been restored to its original condition. From its ramparts, the impressive Liverpool skyline is seen at its best and inside is an Arthur Askey of a museum – small yet perfectly formed!

Perch Rock Fort

The Three Graces seen from across the Mersey.

Pier Head and The Three Graces

This area is now the focus for many of Liverpool's museums, including the Beatles Story, the northern arm of the Tate Gallery, plus the world famous Maritime Museum and the War Rooms associated with the organising of the Atlantic Convoys. It is very appropriate that there should be a Tate Gallery because although Tate was born in Chorley, he made his fortune from importing raw sugar from the West Indies and processing it in Liverpool.

If the Beatles are the Fab Four, then equally famous are the Three Graces which were the buildings so beloved by American visitors as they looked at the Liverpool landscape from the deck of ocean-going liners. The three graces in question are not Faith, Hope and Charity but the Mersey Docks and Harbour Board Building, the Royal Liver Building and the Cunard offices.

The Docks and Harbour Board Building was opened in 1907 and its cathedral-dome dominated the skyline. The Royal Liver Building was completed in 1910 and unashamedly challenged the New York skyline. It was the first multi-storey building to successfully use reinforced concrete. Two huge clock towers, topped with domes on which perch liver birds, are visible for miles out to sea, which was the reason why they were so designed. The Cunard offices were completed during the early years of the First World War and, from 1916, ships from all over the world have been greeted by the Three Graces.

Pilkies

Dominating the history of St Helen's is the glass-making company of Pilkington's who developed as early as 1773. Until recently they were the world's largest glassmakers and are still a successful company. It was here that sheet glass used in shop windows was first rolled out whilst high-quality optical glass was produced for use in scientific instruments and lighthouses. One reason for the firm being established on Merseyside was the availability of high grade sand around the Mersey estuary.

The history of glass throughout the ages is depicted within the splendidly appointed Glass Museum. Admission and car parking is free.

Port Sunlight

The spiritual home of the now world famous Lever (now Unilever) Company has its origins in Bolton born Thomas Hesketh Lever. Beginning as a grocer, he developed a brand of soap and knew well how to market it. Under the name of Sunlight Soap the profits rolled in and he built a factory at Warrington but this was still too far from the sea for the ambitious and philanthropic genius.

He bought land at Bebington on the Mersey and built his factory and the

modern village which he appropriately called Port Sunlight and which survives today in all its glory. The factory was constructed to the highest specifications, and houses with gardens were provided for his workers, as well as an entertainment area. It was here that The Beatles played their first gig, with their new drummer, one Ringo Starr.

The site now also houses the Lady Lever Art Gallery and an excellent information centre. Port Sunlight is also used for film sets, and scenes from the classic *Chariots of Fire* were shot here. Lever, a lad who spoke Lankie twang, deserves to swank that he was also an honorary Scouser.

Lady Lever's Art Gallery.

Speke Hall and Airport

Now run by the National Trust, this magnificent 15th-century half-timbered hall is situated close to Speke (now the John Lennon) airport and has a café and an excellent bookshop, plus strolls around the only stretch of natural woodland remaining on the Liverpool bank of the Mersey. It is also the starting point for a really Magical Mystery Tour which takes in the former homes of the young Paul

McCartney and John Lennon, as well as places such as Penny Lane and Strawberry Fields which really do exist and which inspired the dynamic duo's songs.

Speke airport, as it was then called, began life as early as the 1930s and by the 1950s large crowds would gather to watch the planes taking off and landing. Speke was at its busiest during the Second World War when aircraft arrived in crated parts on board ships from America, that were then conveyed to the airfield to be assembled and flown off to do battle. A docker helping to unload the American bombers, and with the Blitz of his city still fresh in his mind, wrote on one of the containers, 'Aim for their bloody chippies and pubs'.

Liverpool Town Hall

Few buildings in Britain can have engaged the brains of such major architects as that of Liverpool Town Hall. It was first designed in 1749 by John Wood the Elder. The growing civic pride of Liverpool was such that when the building was badly damaged by fire in 1795 no expense was spared to engage the services of James Wyatt, who had carried out impressive restoration work inside Westminster Abbey. This was Georgian architecture at its very best and when Edward VII visited the town hall he compared it very favourably to St Petersburg's Winter Palace in Russia. The building is often open to the public and is one of the jewels in Liverpool's crown.

Toxteth

Too much time has been spent by the national media on the Toxteth riots of the early 1980s and not enough praising one of its illustrious inhabitants whose scientific findings were of world importance.

Jeremiah Horrocks who was born in Toxteth in 1618 and educated at the chapel of Toxteth (which still stands) well deserves his memorial in Westminster Abbey but also needs to have more fuss made of him in his native Liverpool.

In 1639 Horrocks was the curate of the church at Much Hoole on the road between Liverpool and Preston. In Carr House where he lodged and which still stands he predicted the transit of Venus across the face of the sun. So what, you might say, but his mathematical ability meant that he could calculate the distance of the earth from the sun. He also calculated details of the moon's motion as well as predicting the orbits of the planets of Jupiter and Saturn.

This 'Sun of Scouse' brought the name of Horrocks and Toxteth to the very forefront of astronomical thinking.

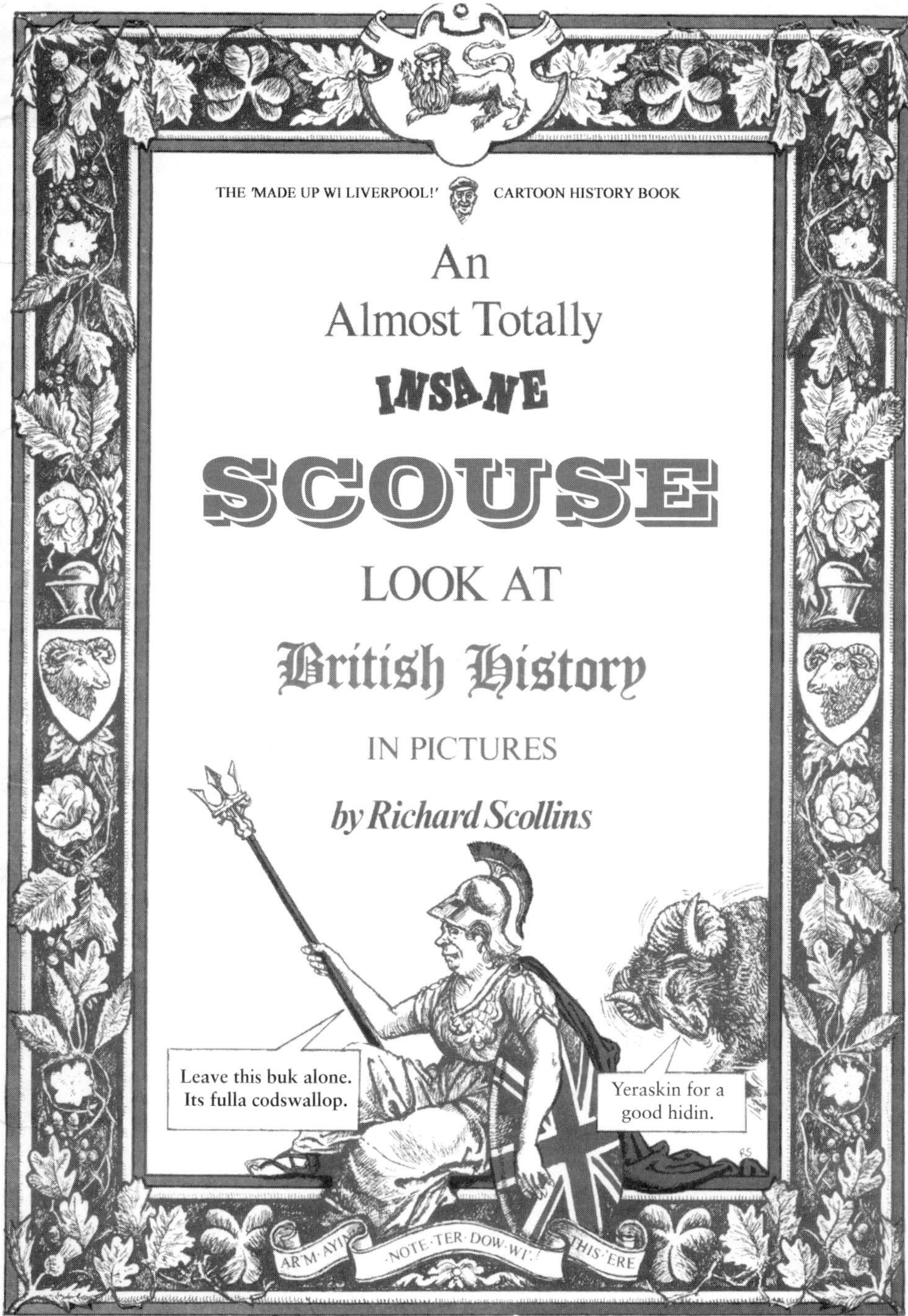
THE 'MADE UP WI LIVERPOOL!' CARTOON HISTORY BOOK
An Almost Totally INSANE SCOUSE LOOK AT British History IN PICTURES
by Richard Scollins
Leave this buk alone. Its fulla codswallop.
Yeraskin for a good hidin.
AR'M·AYIN' ·NOTE·TER·DOW·WI'· THIS·'ERE

Yer 'eddin fer a hidin.
Luke at me wet nellies!

Promise I dint
lerrum burn
purposely.

Alfred and the Cakes – 878

Canute Demonstrates His Inability to Turn the Tide – AD 1020

Ya sed we'd gerra good goz frumeer!

Tross yew ter pick wrong sidev the street!

Howed I know she were goin ter ride side-saddle?

Lady Godiva – AD 1057

The Death of William Rufus – 1100

King John and Magna Carta – 1215

Edward I Presents His Son as Prince of Wales – 1284

YOO-OO ...
'ENRY!

Use scored
agen boss!

Henry VIII and Anne Boleyn – 1529

Raleigh and the Puddle – 1581

Frank , Frank!
Spaniards're comin!

Lerrum wait!

Francis Drake Goes Bowling – 1588

The First Night of 'Hamlet' – 1601

Lissen Whackers, I know it lukes dodgy burri can explain orl onit.

GUN PAIRDER

The Gunpowder Plot – 1605

The Execution of Charles I – 1649

Shift yer bum!

Gerrof will yer!

Mek rume yadivvi!

Shut yer bonechute. Thur's gerrin closer!

Charles II and Friends Hide From the Roundheads – 1651

Isaac Newton Discovers Gravity – 1666

Yer never sed them ud be big girls blouses in skirts!

WE WANNT CHARLIE!

Bonnie Prince Charlie Arrives in Scotland – 1745

Nelson at Trafalgar – 1805

I don' no th' ffect on th' enemy but they scurr mi to death, speshly the big ogly bogger in th' front!

Ooar'im, yons a tattie ed from Birken'ed!

Wellington Inspects His Troops – 1815

Stanley Greets Dr Livingstone – 1871

Twas ace in rehearsal!

TONIGHT'S
ROYAL ENTERTAINER
MR
BERT BARTLEBERRY
OF
BELPER
JUGGLER &
STRONGMAN

Queen Victoria 'Not Amused' – 1878

END OF.